High Lonesome

Cowboy Poetry

Bill Bunting
(Three Feathers)

High Lonesome
Copyright © 2018
Bill (Three Feathers) Bunting

ALL RIGHTS RESERVED
No Portion on this publication may be reproduced, stored in any electronic system, or transmitted in any form or by any means, electronic, mechanical, photocopy, recording, or otherwise, without written permission from the author. Brief quotations may use in literary reviews.

Cover art by Bill (*Three Feathers*) Bunting

ISBN: 978-1-7327807-0-5
First Printing: October 2018

FOR MORE INFORMATION CONTACT

Three Feathers
Bill Bunting
P.O. Box 63
Springfield, CO. 81073
719-529-0729

Please visit our website at
www.artatthreefeathers.com
Online ordering is available for all products

Printed in the USA by
Morris Publishing®
3212 E. Hwy. 30 • Kearney, NE 68847
800-650-7888 • www.morrispublishing.com

"I have found,
as a whole,
Lonesome's good
For a cowboy's soul"

- Three Feathers

TABLE OF CONTENTS

High Lonesome	Pg. 6
Grandma	Pg. 8
Salty Dog	Pg. 10
End of Age	Pg. 13
Fine Line	Pg. 14
Doc	Pg. 16
Thunder	Pg. 20
Breaking' Dawn	Pg. 23
Cowboy Love Poem	Pg. 24
Shorty	Pg. 26
Little Joe	Pg. 28
Love for The Land	Pg. 33
Memories	Pg. 34
The Old Fence	Pg. 36
Bar D Corral	Pg. 38
Wild Cows	Pg. 42
Twister Gray	Pg. 46
Younger Folk	Pg. 48
Blind Lady	Pg. 50

TABLE OF CONTENTS

The Line	Pg. 52
Spirit of The Plains	Pg. 55
Mexican Magician	Pg. 56
Genie	Pg. 57
'Ole Bossy	Pg. 58
Sound of the Wind	Pg. 60
Horse Kissin' Lips	Pg. 66
Hunters Ed	Pg. 68
Pablo and Juanita	Pg. 70
An 'Ole Friend	Pg. 72
Symphony of Silence	Pg. 74
El Perro	Pg. 76
Self Portrait	Pg. 78
The Elevator	Pg. 80
The Drought of 02'	Pg. 82
Riding for the Brand	Pg. 86
The Blessing	Pg. 88
About the Author	Pg. 90

High Lonesome

He talked of what he called the High Lonesome
Where a man could ride all day alone
And the power poles stopped five miles away
And so did the telephone

The road was just ruts 'cross the prairie
Dropped down to the canyon below
Too muddy when it rained in the summer
Too deep when blown full of snow

He told me how he hated man's progress
He never fit in though he'd tried
Now even though he's punchin' another man's cattle
He has the High Lonesome to ride

I asked about the lonely on the Lonesome
He said he wouldn't want it any other way
'Cause if you want the freedom of ridin' the Lonesome
Then lonely is the price you must pay

He told of the house in the canyon
More than likely it was just a line shack
Of the wife he had met in the city
Who had left and hadn't come back

And he told me how she had left him
And I listened to what he said
How she'd fell in love with the cowboy
And the romance of the lifestyle he'd led

But the life starts loosin' it's romance
When you're calvin' at twenty below
And you ain't got your mail in over a month
'Cause the trails drifted in the snow

And there's no one at all to talk to
Just your man and he don't have much to say
You see he's use to ridin' the Lonesome
And he's grown to like it that way

A woman can find herself a talkin'
To the chickens in the yard
'Cause life for a woman on the Lonesome
Can sometimes be mighty hard

So, if you're thinkin' of the High Lonesome
As a place you'd like to ride
Few men have been able to do it
Though many there's been who have tried

You've got to be at peace with your maker
And be at peace with yourself as well
Then maybe you can ride the Lonesome
It's only time that will tell

But, if you're thinkin' of bringin' a woman to the Lonesome
I not sure it's ever been done
And you're thinkin' this one is different
That she'll be the very first one

Well, make sure she's in love with the Lonesome
Where a woman spends all day alone
And the power poles stop five miles away
And so does the telephone

Grandma

The family was all gathered
Which is some family's way
And smoking was the topic
Of discussion that day

And we were trying to decide
If smoking were a sin
We almost had a brawl break out
Right there amongst our kin

Now Grandma was an angel
A real pearl in our eyes
She'd always been there to kiss our hurts
And hug away our cries

Age had lined Grandmas face
And wrinkles all the more
Behind those lines and wrinkles
Great wisdom was held in store

Her hair was sparkling silver
Her smile as bright as day
The family always listened
To what Grandma had to say

So we asked our Grandma
Who was sitting there
Quietly knitting as she rocked
In her rocking chair

She put something in her lip
And packed it in once more
Then leaning forward and through her teeth
She spat towards the door

She gave us her opinion
As we all knew she would
"It's got to be a sin
To burn something that tastes this good"

Salty Dog

The night was dark as an abandoned mine
Clouds obscured the moon
He'd just gunned down two more men
In the Salty Dog Saloon

He was a known killer
Mighty quick with his gun
Some say he started with the law
And now he killed for fun

Both men had taken two rounds
From the 45 on his hip
And you could cover both bullet holes
With a poker chip

Now he was headin' out of town
One step ahead of the law
Although they brought it on themselves
He was the first to draw

And he was ridin' in the night
As dark as it could be
Trustin' in the horse he rode
To dodge the rock and tree

When up ahead he saw a campfire glow
Shining through the night
Although he knew he should ride on
It was a welcome sight

A man squatted there beside the fire
Dressed darker than the night
His eyes they seemed to glow pale green
Reflected by the light

A cigar stuck between his teeth
A bottle in his hand
He seemed to fade into the night
As he arose to stand

The gunman watched the darkness
Where he seen the green eyes glow
He says, "Mister, what do you call yourself?
This I need to know"

He said. "They call me Satan or the Devil
Lucifer of course
Now cowboy you done rode your last
Get down off that horse"

"Cause you been ridin' for my brand
And puttin' on quite a show
This night we're callin' this game quits
To Hell with me you'll go"

Well the gunman drew the only thing
That he had grown to trust
A slick and tuned Colt 45
Free of dirt and rust

Six times he squeezed the trigger
Six deadly bullets fly
To bury deep within the chest
Of a man who will not die

He felt a cold hand on his neck
As he was jerked into the air
The gates of Hell opened beneath him
Flames leaping everywhere

The posse rode upon him
There at the break of day
Underneath the cottonwood
Where his body lay

The signs showed his horse had spooked
Under a cotton tree
His neck was broke by a cottonwood limb
It was plain to see

But the soles of his handmade boots
Were charred by fire or flame
And the cuffs of his Levis
Were burnt by the same

And the empty pistol by his side
Was hard to understand
And six bullets in a cottonwood stump
You could cover with your hand

End of an Age

I'll ride free no more forever
I heard the old cowboy say
Like those who've gone on before me
I'll hang up my spurs today

'Cause times they are a changin'
They're fencin' off the range
I reckon I'm too old
Or maybe too stubborn to change

The longhorns replaced by the hereford
The old chuckwagons parked for good
Settin' lonely out there on the prairie
Just weathered and rotten old wood

Like the Indian and the buffalo before me
Forever no more will they roam
These mountains and prairies and badlands
That once they called their home

Some say this is progress
Others say its just how things are
But I wonder why we would want it
And how is it we've come this far

And I reckon it's easy to see
We've come to the end of an age
This chapter in life's book is over
But it's sure hard to turn the next page

Fine Line

I wrote this poem in the middle of the night after dreamin' about
my kids who had left with their mother several years before.

I rode my pony through the yard
Like many a time before
Watchin' the boy that was playin'
In the dirt beside the front door

But somethin' strange was goin' on
I couldn't understand it you see
Though I could see that boy plain as day
It's like he couldn't see me

I stepped down out of my saddle
Tied my horse and started inside
I was feelin' that good kind a feelin'
You get from an early spring ride

I spoke to the boy as I walked by him
But he never raised his head
He just went on about his playin'
Like he never heard a word that I said

The woman was there in the kitchen
I spoke as I walked through the door
But she never looked up, nor did the girl
Who was playin' with a doll on the floor

Oh, she was laughin' and squealin'
It was music to my ear
But somethin' is wrong with this picture
They don't seem to know that I'm here

The woman is humming a tune to herself
As she busies herself with the meal
A tune that brings back old memories
And feelin's I'd rather not feel

Though I'm standin' right there in the kitchen
They still don't know that I'm there
She sets only three plates at the table
Or maybe she just doesn't care

Well, the smell of the food in the oven
The feel of a fresh spring day
Then in a flicker it seemed to be over
As quickly they faded away

It's just like it was years before
They were gone in an instant it seemed
Once again I'm alone and a wonderin'
Is this real or have I just dreamed

Well, this old house is shore lonesome
The kids, I guess they're most grown
Other than that dog and the horse in the yard
I reckon I'm livin' alone

But I think of home and a family
And the things that I've just seen
Of love and hate, together and alone
And the fine line we walk in between

Doc

His hair was gray
    And his legs were bowed
His old horse he turned out
    He no longer rode

And he had little interest
    In things of today
But he talked of the past
    Times driftin' away

He sat in a rocker
    With a cane by his side
And the days that he talked of
    Were days he could still ride

"You remember old Bob
    It must have been oh round '27 . '28
He rode that ole' buckskin
    Tied him there by the gate"

Though most of this happened
    Seventy years ago
Why I wasn't even born yet
    But I never told him so

He was talkin' of his life
    Of days long gone
And I'd smile and I'd nod
    So the story'd go on

He'd talk of the years
    Of the rain and the drouth
The turnin' of seasons
    The bird's flyin' south

"Remember that hoss trader
Folks called him Slim
Rode in here a few times
From over around Kim"

"Traded some horses
Wanted the bay that he rode
Had some cow in him
And it sure enough showed"

"Heard he got shot
Over Trinidad way
For years I have wondered
What happened to that bay"

"Well the grass is shore good
The best I have seen
The calves are all fat
'Bout ready to wean"

"Guess I won't be in on
The gather this year
'Bout all I can ride
Is this rockin' chair here"

He'd sigh and relax
His breathin' get deep
With a smile on his face
He'd drift off to sleep

Now the day it has come
As we all knew it would
When he told his last story
Closed those old eyes for good

The place he is goin'
    He'll no longer be old
The summer'll be cool
    The winter not cold

His string of horses
    Seems to have no end
He can ride the canyons he loved
    With his brothers again

I can hear him tellin' stories
    As he's ridin' up there
"Remember the time we roped the buck
    Then tried for the bear"

"Look here comes 'Ole Slim
    I'd know that boy well
But I sure thought all horse traders
    Were headed to hell"

"Look at him ridin' there
    He's shore lookin' fine
If he's got bullet holes in him
    I shore don't see no sign"

"He's ridin' that bay
    That I wanted so bad
I'd wondered what happened
    To that horse that he'd had"

"Boys let's ride for that bunkhouse
    And call it a day
If horse trading's allowed here
    I'll be ridin' that bay"

God in his wisdom
    And his glory so grand
Kept a place there in heaven
    For a broken cow hand

He can ride out eternity
    On the horse of his choice
When I listen real close
    I can still hear his voice

"A hand there from Clayton
    Rode into the place
A little sorrel mare
    A blaze on her face"

"Can't remember the year
    Reckon I was about 16
Thought that mare was the best horse
    I'd ever seen"

"Can't remember his name
    How 'bout you
That mare had gone lame
    Thrown a front shoe"

Thunder

He's there in the rest home
Crazy they say
Thinks he was some kinda' gunman
Back in his day

"They think that I'm crazy
Like it's some kind of joke
But they never heard the whine of the bullet
Or the smell of the smoke"

"Or the smell of the dust
In the street at high noon
Or dancin' the dance
Of a six-gun tune"

"The buck of the pistol
In the palm of your hand
When the talkin's all over
You've made your stand"

"The star on your vest
Shinin' bright in the sun
As you see his hand dart
To the butt of his gun"

"And it's life and it's death
In the blink of the eye
In the dust of the street
Which one's gonna die"

"Look at those horse's boy
As they ride across the sky
Right there in the sunset
As evening draws nigh"

"Look at the men boy
I killed each one
They're waitin' for me out there
When my days here are done"

"I done all my shootin'
From the right side of the law
But my hands are so crippled
Don't think I can draw"

"But they look the same
As the day that they died
They're going to draw me and quarter me
And tan this old hide"

"At the foot of the bed
There's a badge in that chest
When my days here are done
Pin it here on my vest"

"There's a pistol rolled up
In an old oily rag
Would you lay it beside me
Right here 'gainst my leg"

"And I'll be ready to take
What they have in store
I'll made my stand in the middle
Of the street once more"

A crazy old man
In the home for the old
A crazy old story
The old man told

But I was drawn to him
    I was there on the day
When death came upon him
    And he passed away

And there in the chest
    And the foot of his bed
Was the tarnished old badge
    Just like he had said

I unrolled the old pistol
    From out of the rag
And I put it beside him
    Right next to his leg

Is that thunder I hear
    As a storm draws nigh
Or are they havin' that shoot out
    Up there in the sky

Breakin' Dawn

Lord, it's shore a pretty mornin'
Just now breakin' dawn
The grass out here on the prarie
Is as green as city folk's lawn

The meadow lark's starting to sing
As the night critters scurry and hide
It's just me out here on the prairie
Me and this 'ole horse that I ride

A coyote yips a final tune
As a hush falls 'cross the land
A hush so calm and quiet
Stilled by the Master's hand

And Lord, I smell a million wild roses
Their fragrance enhanced by the dew
As I ride out here 'cross the prairie
Just me, this 'ole horse and you

And Lord, I see you in all your creation
I hear your voice in the wind
Huh, cattle tracks through this hole in the fence
Looks like I've got fence here to mend

Lord this must be a whole lot like heaven
It's shore 'nuff good to be alive
The suns just a red ball there in the east
And it looks like I've got cattle to drive

Cowboy Love Poem

The first time that she saw him
It was love at first sight
And she dreamed of him
Most near every night

She dreamed so often about him
He was so big and strong
She dreamed someday he'd sweep her off her feet
And carry her along

Each time that she saw him
He just seemed to pass her by
Why if he had only looked at her
She felt that she would die

Her mom warned her about him
He's just not our kind
Nothin' but heartache awaits you
If you two become entwined

Her father only snorted
     Had nothin' more to say
She could tell by his actions
     His blessings were not on the way

So she schemed and dreamed like Juliet
     To meet her Romeo
Although their love was forbidden
     She felt that she must go

So she slipped away to meet him
     In the dark of the night
And there in the distance
     She saw the glow of his light

Well, they met on the bridge at midnight
     They'll meet no more a-gain
She a southbound heifer
     He a northbound train

Shorty

"No need to bring your trailer
    You leave your horse at home
We have one we'll let you ride"
    He told me on the phone

"We need to make a gather
    And bring our cattle in
Put them on some milo stalks
    They're getting' mighty thin"

When I got there I looked around
    To see which horse was mine
"We'll let you ride 'Ole Shorty
    You'll get along just fine"

Now Shorty was half Shetland
    And a poor example of that breed
Although I think he saw himself
    As a fair and noble steed

Now I wouldn't say 'Ole Shorty's short
    He's just a might petite
I shined my boots on the buffalo grass
    And got cactus in my feet

One of them old Brangus cows
    She sure got on the prod
Rip and snort and carryin' on
    Tearin' up the sod

She was pawin' dirt and blowin' snot
    And causin quite a stir
And from where I sat and Shorty stood
    We both looked up to her

Now I'd grown fond of Shorty
    And the spirit that he had
And I was right concerned for us
    'Cause this old cow was mad

So I whispered in 'Ole Shorty's ear
    Admidst the snot and flyin' dust
"You run one way, I'll the other
    She won't get both of us"

Little Joe

Little Joe came to work for us
    When he was just a big ole' kid
We grew him up fast, cowboy style
    And I can't say I'm sorry we did

Like when you are leavin' a pasture with an electric fence
    And he gets out to shut the gate
A man could be cruel and hard hearted
    And just set in the pickup and wait

But me not bein' that sort of fellow
    And knowin' what I should do
I backed the trailer up a ways
    To save him a step or two

And when he touched that door handle
    His squall almost brought tears
Somehow the trailer had rolled into the fence
    The whole pickup is hot it appears

Then, "We'll let you ride Ole' Brownie
    You'll do fine, he's kid broke of course"
Next week we sold Brownie to a stock contractor
    He's a world class buckin' horse

Little Joe took all this learnin'
    With such ease and grace
He never said much about it
    Just a silly ole' grin on his face

"Why, that cows only bluffin'
    Stay put with your feet in place"
But he decided to cut and run
    When she started blowin' snot in his face

And he slipped in his haste to exit
Arms out to brace his fall
His front end downhill, his rear in the air
When she rolled him into a ball

Now we all thought Little Joe had a sense of humor
He'd just smile and go on his way
But that smile was him thinkin' of gettin' even
He was dreamin' of the hour and the day

Well, they said Little Joe had grown to be a good cowboy
Though I hadn't seen him in a number of years
Then we both went to work on the Flying W
They were runnin' some yearlin' steers

"Now that one looks a little puny"
And this is how we earned our pay
I was feelin' right generous
I says, "Joe you can rope this one today"

'Cause I'd been doin' all the ropin'
I'd just rope them and set on my horse
Little Joe had done all the doctorin'
He'd drew the short end of course

So he threw a loop 'round his horns
He turned back and he hit with a crash
I was out of my saddle and upon him
Like Superman there in a flash

29

But that steer came to his feet like he was loco
His eyes were evil and mean
His front end blowin' nothin' but snot
His back end nothin' but green

With a bellow handed down from his ancestors
And a hatred handed down from the past
He has evil intentions on my body
And man that ole' steers comin' fast

So I sprinted in the opposite direction
I could see there was only one hope
This was a race with only one winner
I had to beat him to the end of that rope

And, ooh I should be nearin' the end of it
Ooh he's blowin' buggers up my back
Then I glanced over my shoulder at my partner
With that grin on his face pitchin' slack

Perhaps the greatest wisdom a man can have is to know when not to break the silence

- Three Feathers

The drouth and dust of the prairie is far better for a man's soul than rain-soaked asphalt and concrete

-Three Feathers

Love for the Land

I wrote this poem about my dad who at ninety four years is still on
the ranch grandad homesteaded in 1915 on the high plains of
Southeastern Colorado.

The lifestyle he is livin'
Few men understand
As he coaxes a living from the land

His roots like his crops are deep
In that prairie soil
Planted by his ancestors
Through blood and sweat and toil

Honest men of character
Who stood when called to stand
Driven by hard work and faith
And a Love for the Land

Memories

"What's that your lookin' at Pops"
    As he stared in the evenin' sky
And I took my kerchief from my pocket
    And wiped a tear from his eye

His flowin' mustache, a snowy white
    Spread' 'cross his weathered face
The left side had a little twitch
    Where the stroke had left its trace

He said, "Cowboyin' just ain't the same
    As it was there in the past
I tell you son this way of life
    Is ending mighty fast"

"Why when Pete and I rode the Pecos
    A fence was hard to find"
And I saw his horse kickin' up dust
    In the memories of his mind

"Pablo and I rode the Cimarron and Crease
    Rode for the JJ Brand
Why he wasn't much over five foot tall
    But he was quite a hand"

"Rode the canyons there in Utah
    The Sawtooth in Idaho
It was ridin' up the Green there in Wyomin'
    I run across Ol' Joe"

"And Joe and me rode for years and years
    From Canada to Mexico
Whenever we go the urge
    We'd just pack up and go"

"There weren't any fences
We rode free as the wind
Stampede there in Texas
Where Joe met his end"

"And Pete, he drowned in Kansas
Rode his horse into quicksand
Pablo died in New Mexico
A pistol in his hand"

"That you Joe," he looked at me
Once more those old eyes shined
And I saw his horse kickin' up dust
In the memories of his mind

"Joe. Look Here. Here comes Ol' Pete
Bob and Pablo too
Pablo, me amigo, it's been awhile
Since I rode the Crease with you"

"Boys remember when we rode wild and free
Now somethin's sure gone wrong
Cowboyin' ain't what it used to be
I guess I've lived too long"

"Boys, lite and sit and stay awhile
These days a good cowboys hard to find"
And he closed his eyes and rode his horse
Through the memories in his mind

The Old Fence

One of the roads we travel on a somewhat frequent basis leads us past an
eastern Oklahoma ranch with a couple a miles of white painted fences.
Over the years I've watched the gradual decline of the fence. It stirs me
to imagine.

The paint's a' pealin'
Boards have fell down
The old fence ain't been painted
Since the kids moved to town

Things didn't go
According to our dreams
Shore hard to make a livin'
On the land now it seems

Expenses go up
Income goes down
The old fence ain't been painted
Since the kids moved to town

But Ma and I are happy
It's quiet out here
And it shore is pretty
This time a' year

The redwoods are bloomin'
The meadows so green
Why it's one of the prettiest mornins'
I've ever seen

But Ma and I are happy
With the things we've got
Though the boards on the fence
Are startin' to rot

The dew on the grass
     Looks like jewels on a crown
The old fence ain't been painted
     Since the kids moved to town

But things didn't go
     The way Ma and I had planned
The kid's would marry, have families
     And work on the land

But it's hard to make a livin'
     I'll tell you for shore
I really can't blame them
     For wantin' more

The white on the fence
     Is turnin' to brown
The old fence ain't been painted
     Since the kids moved to town

Sittin' on the porch
     It's quiet out here
Shore is pretty
     This time a' year

Ma and I are happy
     Though it's just us two
We have faith in the Lord
     That He'll see us through

But I shore miss the kids
     And I hope they're ok
Lord could I ask you
     To bless them today

I can see a spot
     Where a boards fallen down
The old fence ain't been painted
     Since the kids moved to town

Bar D Corral

We were brandin' some cattle
At the south Bar D Corral
That night we lit a campfire
Things were goin' mighty well

When an old cowboy rode into camp
In the darkness shouted, "Hello"
Then he squatted at our campfire
Took some coffee and sipped it slow

It's like he rode in from nowhere
Where he come from no one's sure
But he smelled of sage and cedar
Wood smoke and horse manure

Not that nasty, dank and rank 'ole smell
Like to some of you it'd seem
But clean and fresh and clear
Like in a cowboy's dream

He said, "I've been ridin' 'cross this land
And I'll tell you boys for shore
Things just ain't the same
As they were once before"

"'Cause there's concrete and barb wire
　　　　And asphalt on the trail
Why a man a ridin' horseback
　　　　Can wind up in jail"

"'Cause there's laws and rules and speed limits
　　　　Things I don't understand
And I don't know what it has to do
　　　　With the makin's of a man"

"And the ranches are thirty acres
　　　　Not enough to run one horse
But they're all fenced and posted
　　　　You can't ride through of course"

"And all this high-powered horse flesh
　　　　Men sure take lots of pride
Why I've had rangy old half mustangs
　　　　That I'd sooner ride"

"And your campfire's shore invitin'
　　　　Though it just ain't the same
As when we drove longhorns up the trail
　　　　Now it's more like a game"

And I looked across the campfire
Into those tired old eyes
And I got a glimpse of his memories
And I came to realize

That time's they are a changin'
This it is for shore
And things just ain't the same
As they were once before

And I'll never forget the words he said
As he stepped into the saddle
He said, "All I've known all my life
Is horses, mules, and cattle"

"But I hear they play harps in heaven
And there's days I hear their tune
So, I know my days are numbered
And I'll be goin' soon"

"Look at all this land around me
Land I've grown to love
There's just one thing I ask
Of the Lord up above"

"That there ain't no fences in heaven
So, I'll feel hemmed in
So, I can ride free
On the range once again"

Then he swung into the saddle
And rode into the night
Though not a track we could find
With the comin' of light

And times they are a changin'
This it is for shore
And thing's will never be the way
They were once before

So, it's with songs and stories and poems
We remember the past
And the words that we speak
May be all that will last

And I too look at the land
That I've grown to love
And I too ask the Lord
Up there above

That when the final gathers made
And the sortin' is all through
May I have a ranch there in heaven
With a pony or two

But just don't let there be any fences
So, I'll feel hemmed in
So, I too can ride free
On the range once again

Wild Cows

The history of the cow in the southern states of America dates back to the early 1500's with several Andalusia cattle being brought to New Spain by Spanish explorers. Later in the same century Spanish explorers searching for gold drove along large herds of Spanish cattle as a walking supply of fresh meat.

As all cattle are prone to do, these cattle strayed or were abandoned and soon were running wild. Their numbers rapidly increased and soon the brush country was full of cattle running wild and free and unbranded. These cattle gave many a soldier returning from the Civil War a chance at a fresh start.

Wild Cows

All day in the saddle
    Swingin' his rope at wild cattle
And stickin' his brand on their hide

They were doin' right well
    In this brushy, thorny hell
His partner always by his side

The brush was awful thick
    And the cattle full of tick
But they were free for the takin'

A loop 'round their horns
    Tied to a tree of thorns
Irons heated in the fire he's a makin'

Then it's back there in that tangle
    Where the thorns will cut and mangle
Regardless if it's man or it's beast

He carries his loop ready
    As he sits his pony steady
His partner workin' to the east

Then out of the brush
    The steer made that final rush
With only one intent on his mind

With a bellow from hell
    That the cowboy knew so well
He would tangle with the first thing he could find

As he heard those horns rattle
And he turned in his saddle
He realized he was too late

To escape the wrath
Of this longhorn in his path
He would now have to settle for his fate

Then through the brush a blur
Came a black and yellow cur
And took the horn intended for him

He lay there on the grass
And he breathed out his last
And the fire in his eyes grew awful dim

His thoughts were not on cattle
As he lay him 'cross his saddle
And slowly led his horse back to camp

And as he dug the grave
For his partner true and brave
His tears turned that dry ground damp

His heart was full of sorrow
As he thought about tomorrow
As he carved the name on that block of stone

They'd always been together
No matter what the weather
And now he'd have to ride that trail alone

Memories of the past
  Came floatin' by real fast
As he laid the rock on that fresh turned sod

But he believed in the hereafter
  And the sound of cowboy's laughter
And the presence of an ever-living God

So with a tear there in his eye
  He turned his face toward the sky
And said, "I don't know if dogs are allowed"

"But if you'd take my pard
  Whose dyin' is so hard
You know that I'd be awful proud"

"We lived our lives alone
  Now he rests beneath that stone
He gave his life for me in the end"

"And I've heard it said
  And in the Word I've read
No greater love than to die for a friend"

Well his day seemed brighter
  And his heart felt a little lighter
As he walked away from the grave that day

If his partners not up there
  Chasin' cows without a care
He must have found a herd along the way

Twister Gray

He sat his horse in the chute
Cowboy hat to boot
He'd drawed a horse called Twister Gray

That 'ole horse could sure buck
And with any luck
He would finish up there in the pay

He measured his bronc rein just right
As they jerked those cinches tight
And he hollered. "Turn him outside"

'Ole Twister came out upside down
Then he twist his body 'round
As he felt the spurs a rakin' on his hide

He stuck his head between his knees
Then purty as you please
He just started to unglue

From the bottom of his heart
That old bronc broke apart
And he tried every trick he ever knew

All four hooves toward the sky
Like he was gonna' fly
Then back to earth with a stiff leg jolt

He'd try to shake that man from the saddle
'Til his bones would almost rattle
But he just couldn't break that cowboy's holt

He plowed a furrow with his nose
While his hind quarters rose
To try to kick the stars from the sky

But Billy had been spurrin' down just right
And he held that bronc rein tight
And he just let 'Ole Twister fly

When that eight second whistle blew
Billy and Twister never knew
So intent was their battle there that night

And Billy rode him to a stop
And 'Ole Twister head it drop
'Cause he knew that he had done lost the fight

As he stood there by his side
He says. "Boys, this bronc is broke to ride
Though he's a tough one, this 'Ole Twister Gray"

And he tipped his hat to the crowd
Who was applaudin' loud
And turned and slowly walked away

As he stood there proud and tall
He heard his mother's call
Above the sound of the other noise

She said "Son that was quite a ride
Now put your rockin' horse aside
And put him with rest of your toys"

Then she said a prayer
As she was standin' there
"Lord, thank you for this little cowboy"

"I never knew boots and a hat
And Levis where he sat
Could bring a mother so much joy"

"And in his life ahead
I'm sure tears will be shed
There always seems to have to be some pain"

"But Lord, help him walk straight and true
And keep his eyes on You
And Lord, would you keep your hand upon his rein"

Younger Folk

I was talkin' to some younger folk
    They seem to think my words a joke
They couldn't understand a word I said

It was like I was a gringo
    And I couldn't speak their lingo
They said "Old man your way of life is dead"

Times are sure a changin' boys
    Music now is more like noise
And men are wearin' sandals on their feet

Why a man would be hard pressed
    To find a hat or leather vest
Among a thousand head on a city street

'Cause you see they never heard of Dodge City
    Trailin' cattle or Miss Kitty
Or the stock yards at the end of the rail

They never heard of ridin' drag
    Or heard an outlaw brag
'Bout the dead men he had left along the trail

They never sat beneath the stars
    Without the sound of cars
Or a stereo blarin' in their ears

Or sat around a fire
    And picked an 'ole guitar
With the thoughts of a sweetheart bringin' tears

They never heard of gatherin' cattle
    Or heard the arrows rattle
Through the cottonwoods as the Kiowas swept by

As crime wrecks their city
    Lord, you know it is a pity
They can't see life through a cowboy's eye

Times are sure a changin' fast
    You and I may be the last
We may be the last ones up the trail

'Cause you see they never heard of Dodge City
    Trailin' cattle or Miss Kitty
Or the stock yards at the end of the rail

The Blind Lady

They'd grown old and she'd gone blind
This rancher and his wife
He'd only drove in the city
A few times in his life

The pickup was battered from years of use
Slowly rusting and fallin' apart
Sometimes he had to short it across
Just to get it to start

Six lanes of traffic headin' east
And he was doin' his best
To find a place to turn around
'Cause he wanted to be goin' west

Now drivin' in this traffic
Was gettin' to be a pain
The honkin' horns and squealin' tires
And now it was startin' to rain

This caused quite a problem
'Cause the wipers wouldn't work
No matter how hard he hit the dash
They wouldn't even jerk

Now this caused quite a dilemma
    Not seein' through the glass
His head stuck out the window
    While cars tried to pass

The harder it rained the louder she prayed
    But it was to no avail
Before she'd finished with her prayer
    It now had started to hail

He came to a stop in the center lane
    As honkin' filled the air
And calmly said to his blind wife
    As though without a care

"I don't think the Lord is hearin'
    What it is you're sayin'
You scoot over and drive a while
    And let me do the prayin'"

The Line

"I've rode the line for years
Now it appears
They say I'm gettin' too old"

"This ride is my last
My time it is past
The winters are gettin' too cold"

As he spoke
To the dog, he awoke
And he reached down to scratch his head

With one cocked ear
As is to hear
Every word the old man said

"It's cold today
But there's no other way
I'd rather spend it you know"

"Though its cold out here
The Lord draws near
And it's just now startin' to snow"

"It's the life I've chose
And I suppose
Folks get along in town just fine"

"Though my bones are old
        And sometimes they're cold
I'd rather die on the line"

"I'll gather our tack
        And make us a pack
And saddle 'Ole Buck in the shed"

"It's twenty below
        And startin' to snow
Let's go for a ride" he said

When spring rolled around
        He's not to be found
Buck and the dogs gone too

His saddle and tack
        Are gone from the shack
And it was plain to all us who knew

That this ride was his last
        'Cause his time was past
Though this was his life and his love

And we all had a fear
        Of the news we would hear
As we searched the hill's up above

But no body is found
No bones on the ground
Though we watched each day as we rode

A flash in the trees
It's only the breeze
He and 'Ole Buck never showed

A year has passed
It's winter at last
And I ride to that old line shack

There is a note
Someone has wrote
On a piece of brown paper sack

Say's "All's goin' well
From this note you should tell
Me and Buck and the dogs doin' fine"

"It's twenty below
And startin' to snow
Greetings from here on the line"

Spirit of The Plains
(Ode to the Buffalo)

From eons past he ruled the land
      From and undisputed throne
Made from natures finest
      Of earth and grass and stone

The prairie was his kingdom
      Seemed to stretch without end
His anthem softly playing
      On the ceaseless wind

Then a new sound was heard across the kingdom
      It was the wind of change
A sound never heard before
      A sound so harsh and strange

Now his kingdom is divided
      As man staked off his claim
There's a new king on the prairie
      And progress is his name

Though his kingdom is divided
      His spirit still remains
You can hear it if you listen
      In the wind upon the plains

You can hear it if you listen
      He's the Spirit of the Plains

Mexican Magician

Bob took Sally on vacation
    Down to Mexico
While they were there they took in
    A Mexican magic show

The magician done a bunch of tricks
    With a deck of cards
Pulled a rope from his empty hand
    Stretched for yards and yards

Then he pulled a rabbit outa' his hat
    And a couple of doves too
Tossed those birds into the air
    And away those doves flew

Then he put a woman in a box
    And sawed her right in half
Told some jokes in Spanish Bob couldn't understand
    Made other folks laugh

Then he told the audience
    How good they had been
And after his final act
    They'd not see him again

He said, "I'll make myself disappear
    At the count of three"
Sally said, "I don't believe it
    This I've got to see"

So he got himself under a blanket
    Got everything in place
Counted, "Uno, dos" POOF he was gone
    Disappeared without a tres

Genie

Bob and Sally had parted ways
    After bein' married about a week
And they weren't real happy
    With each other so to speak

Then Sally found a magic lamp
    Or was it just a jar
Anyway out jumps this genie
    Say's "My names Jiffar"

"And I'll grant you three wishes
    If you ask me real nice
But whatever you ask for
    Old Bob's gonna get it twice"

She said "I'd like a Cadillac
    A bright and shiny blue"
He says "You now have it
    And Bob, he now has two"

She said "I'd like a million bucks
    If its not too much trouble"
He says "You now have it
    And Bob now has its double"

Sally thought for quite a while
    Then took a long deep breath
And said "Mr. Genie would you scare me
    Just scare me half to death"

'Ole Bossy

I have seen cowboys get attached to all kinds of critters.
Everything from poodles to chickens. Sometimes even an old cow.

Her hide hung slack over bony ribs
Patchy hair a brindle gray
She'd been rode hard and put up wet
Was what a cowboy'd say

She walked like she'd been foundered
Hip bones pokin' through her hide
Rather than admit she belonged to them
Most ranchers would have died

Each breath she took started with a gurgle
And wound up with a wheeze
The cough that rattled in her chest
Sometimes drove her to her knees

And when she bawled it was a mournful sound
Brought tears to the toughest eyes
Many a cowboy packed up and left
After hearin' those mournful cries

Her teeth were worn, her ears were short
       Like maybe they'd been froze
She always had a little snot
       A runnin' out her nose

She had a knot in her forehead
       Her eyes were permanently crossed
She held her head off to one side
       She walked like she was lost

My neighbors, they all told me
       They'd get rid of her if they were me
She won't make it through another winter
       You just wait and see

I know she's getting' mighty old
       But I've had her most her life
So I guess I'll keep her one more year
       After all she is my wife

Sound of the Wind

The clock kept tickin' and the calendar turned
     As we started a year brand new
As we heads toward, the year of our Lord
     The year two thousand and two

Now the winter was tame
     Just not the same
And the snow just never fell

The weather was mild
     Like a well-behaved child
They said summers shore gonna' be hell

Now spring rolled around
     No grass to be found
You see it just didn't green

The old timers say
     It's never been this a' way
It's the driest they've ever seen

And the wind blew hard
     Never seemed to grow tired
As dust filled the air

The cattle grew thin
     It hardened the men
You'd hear some cry and some swear

She came from the south
     Never heard of a drought
Where the tall pine timbers grew

Where they baled grass hay
       And it rained every day
And the wind it never blew

Now she'd run wild
       In the woods as a child
And was used to havin' her way

But they fell in love
       With help from above
And were married in the wind one day

She moved to his home
       Where the buffalo roam
On what they call the high plains

Where it'd been a year
       At least right near
Since there'd been any sign of the rains

Oh this land was tough
       The goin' was rough
A land you learned not to fight

And the wind would howl
       Like a wolf on the prowl
It blew both day and night

Once again he's in the saddle
       Sortin' the cattle
More goin' to the market each day

There's no grass at all
       It's comin' on fall
And we're runnin' out of hay

"Lord this drought
        The wind from the south
Oh Lord won't you just let it rain"

"Lord I pray
        This wind every day
Will drive a woman insane"

Sometimes we find
        The winds in our mind
The voices we hear are not real

If you listen my friend
        To the sound of the wind
You can't trust the things that you feel

You see the wind is a lie
        And it's going to try
To deceive you if it can

Hang onto the Word
        And the truth that you've heard
And stand firm beside your man

He showed her true love
        Faith from above
Tryin' to be a husband and a friend

But she wouldn't try
        All she heard was the lie
As she listened to the sound of the wind

The stress of the drought
        The pull of the south
And the wind that blew each day

And in the end
       It was the wind
That blew the woman away

Now the drought it has broke
       Like some kinda' joke
Spring flowers are bloomin' this late

The winds just a breeze
       Getting' close to a freeze
Some say it's the Lord, some fate

So he's taken a holt
       He's workin' this colt
In the round pen here today

Tryin' to forget the past
       It happened so fast
And the wind that blew the woman away

Sometimes we find
       The winds in our mind
The voices we hear are not real

If you listen my friend
       To the sound of the wind
You can't trust the things that you feel

True prosperity is being content with what you have

-Three Feathers

There's no better smell in the world I am sure than smoke from a campfire and fresh horse manure

-Three Feathers

Horse Kissin' Lips

I had a friend that taught his horse to kiss him. His wife wasn't real
taken with this as she seemed to think that it made his mustache
smell funny.

At the edge of night
In the fadin' light
He unsaddled down at the coral

The air was pure
Smelled of fresh horse manure
He'd always liked that smell

He put 'Ole Buck up for the night
Made sure things were alright
When he heard the slam of the old screen door

As he shut the gate
He could hardly wait
To hold her in his arms once more

She met him half way
Says, "I missed you today
More than ever before it seems"

And into his arms
With her womanly charms
Came his wife, the girl of his dreams

Now the moon was shinin' bright
    And the night was right
For a little romance to begin

When she says, "It's easy to tell
    By the way that you smell
That you've been kissin' your horse again"

"Now this may be ok with you
    This thing cowboys do
But somehow you've crossed the line"

With hands on her hips
    She says, "Horse kissin' lips
Just ain't gonna' be kissin' on mine"

He says, "Now this isn't fair
    'Ole Buck doesn't care
Why he doesn't care what I do"

"Not once in his life
    Since you've been my wife
Has he complained about me kissin' you"

Hunters Ed

He'd taken hunters safety course
And he'd learned all the rules
He was smarter than his partners
Which he now considered fools

But he took them all huntin'
In the fall season
To impress them with his intelligence
Was sure part of his reason

And he'd wandered through the brush
On the trail of a white tail buck
And dark was now comin' on
And he hadn't had no luck

And it was plumb embarrassin'
The thing that he now faced
He wasn't sure where he was
And the trail had got misplaced

But he remembered what the book had said
Just stay right where you are
You'll be easier to find
Than if you wander off afar

And if you are in trouble
        Fire three shots into the air
It's a universal signal
        That all outdoors men share

So he sat there on the creek bank
        And fired a three-shot round
He was proud of his education
        He was sure he'd soon be found

He cupped his hand to his ear
        Listenin' for a reply
And when none come he fired three more
        Shots into the sky

Well, they found him three years later
        His bones scattered 'cross the sand
His quiver bare of arrows
        His bow clutched in his hand

Pablo and Jaunita

Pablo and Jaunita had a house
    A casa you might say
And Pablo earned his livin'
    Herdin' sheep every day

Jaunita said,
    "Somethings wrong I theenk
Every night you come home
    With that awful stink"

"And it makes it hard
    For me to go to sleep
When you come to bed
    Smellin' like those stinkin' sheep"

"It wouldn't hurt you to take a bath
    Down there in the creek
It wouldn't hurt you none
    At least every other week"

So she handed Pablo a bar of soap
    And sent him on his way
There wasn't much he could do
    Or much that he could say

So he called his old sheepdog
Says, "Come along Blue
She's blamin' that smell on me
When she's really smellin' you"

"Cause you sleep at the foot of the bed
This will work out you see
I'll give you the scrubbin'
Instead of scrubbing me"

Well, he was right proud
Of the thing that he had done
Though Blue didn't seem
To like that scrubbin' none

But Jaunita said, "This isn't right
The smell is still the same"
And instead of blamin' it on the dog
Ole' Pablo got the blame

Well Blue is sleepin' in his favorite spot
There at the foot of the bed
And Pablo's sleepin' all alone
Down in the lambing shed

An 'Ole Friend

They say he's old and all used up
    His worth is in the past
The end of his useful days
    Is comin' mighty fast

There's just no room for him
    In this society in which we live
Why, he might offend someone
    With the advice he's known to give

The same advice that was sought
    By leaders, kings and queens
From cowboys to congressmen
    Housewives and college deans

Once he roamed far and wide
    Was known throughout the land
Was always there in time of need
    To lend a helpin' hand

But now they say he's dyin'
    Good riddance some would say
But I'm fearful of life without him
    If he should pass away

Our leaders have already deserted him
    As they play the political game
As they trample on the people
    In their quest for power and fame

One of his old sayin's
    Stuff always run downhill
From the leaders to the followers
    The truth is in it still

The bait is laid, the traps been set
    Many have been caught in the snare
Now someone new is in his place
    And he's no longer there

As we gathered 'round him
    It'd sure be hard to see him go
Life here without him
    Might be a tough 'ole row to hoe

And I wonder why so few are gathered
    To mourn his demise
Then I look around us
    And I come to realize

Those who are not mourning with us
    I'll have to say in their defense
Either never knew him or forgot him
    Our 'ole friend Common Sense

Symphony of Silence

Some say he was born
    Two hundred years too late
The product of the union
    When tradition and history mate

The blood of the Irish, the English and the Cherokee
    Run through his veins
He was born to hold a rifle
    And a set of bridal reins

And to see the beauty in the empty
    The desolate and bare
From the mountains to the deserts
    And the melody they share

As he listens to the stanzas
    That few men understand
A symphony of silence
    From an orchestra conducted by the land

The trees give standing ovation
    Clapping tightly silent hands
As the glory of the sunset
    Spreads across the desert sands

It's the chorus of the quiet
    Ever singing seldom heard
By those listening with their hearing
    For an octave or a word

It's the quiet that is the music
    Ringing in his ears
The same quiet sang to his ancestors
    Down throughout the years

To lead them to an empty land
    A place that had been saved
Far beyond the city walls
    Past the roads that had been paved

To dance to the music
    Few men understand
A symphony of silence
    Conducted by the land

And down throughout the ages
    This traditions passed along
Of riding through the empty
    Listening to the silent song

You can tell by the far away look in his eye
    And the firmness of his hand
He's heard the music of the silence
    And he's a member of the band

El Perro

He was just a six week old puppy
    Cow dog through and through
Mostly long haired border collie
    With one eye the right color of blue

He lay on the porch in the sunlight
    And watched an old barn cat stalk away
That old cat walked like he owned the whole ranch
    Some day that cat's gonna' pay

So, he got up to get a drink of cold water
    And stared at the reflection he saw
The distortion there in the water
    "I'm a full blood Chihuahua-wa"

"My head it is to beeg' for my body
    My ears they are too beeg' for my head
I must be a full blood Chihuahua
    No matter what my mudder' has said"

So, he lays back down in the sunlight
    Where puppies like to lay it seems
He lays there with one foot a twitchin'
    Dreamin' those puppy dreams

Oh, si they called him El Perro
    The fastest in all of Mexico
His draw it was queek like the lightin'
    The others they were just much too slow

But he would not drink their tequila
    It makes your eyes awful red
It makes you loco in the cabesa
    Which means you're crazy in the head

But si he was muy hombre
    The senoritas would flock to his side
He'd dance all night in the cantina
    Then off 'cross the prairie he'd ride

In search of the bad man El Gato
    Who was the worst in the land
He swore someday he would get him
    In the dust of the street make his stand

Well, he ran him to the ground in El Paso
    And there in the dust of the street
When the shootin' it was all over
    El Perro had dust on his feet

So, he gathered all El Gato's dinero
    His gold and silver and then
He shared it with all the poor peons
    So, they could buy frijoles again

Well he woke up there in the sunlight
    Watched Ol' Slim walk cross' the yard
He realized he was just a cow dog
    But all this dreamin' had sure made him tired

So, he lay back down in the sunshine
    He's dreamin' those dreams again
He's dreamin' of pretty senoritas
    And all the places he's been

Self Portrait

He was tired of the dust
        And the grit in his beans
Of doctorin' sick cows
        And holes in his jeans

He was tired of the drought
        The mud and the rain
That he needed a change
        Was mighty plain

He'd heard them before
        And thought them a sage
As they told stories and poems
        Up there on the stage

And the life that he'd led
        Had been interestin' and well
He had some stories
        That he could sure tell

He'd get him a bus
        And get him a gig
Like Baxter and Waddie
        He'd make it real big

So he bought him new boots
        A hat with a big brim
In front of the mirror
        He'd squint and he'd grin

And he'd tell those old stories
        With such ease and grace
Using all kinds of expressions
        With his hands and his face

Then he got his first chance
        In front of a crowd
He shined up his boots
        And man was he proud

Of the stories he'd tell
     And the poems he'd say
He'd patiently practiced
     Awaiting this day

He walked on the stage
     In front of the crowd
The applause and the clapping
     Was noisy and loud

Then it became quiet
     Not a sound could he hear
Every eye was upon him
     It soon became clear

Fear knotted his stomach
     And moved to his throat
He forgot the words
     To the poem he'd wrote

He looked at the floor
     Tryin' to remember a line
Then up at the sky
     As if for a sign

Then he pulled a wrinkled paper
     From out of his vest
And he read them the poem
     That he thought the best

His stomach was knotted
     His head had a throb
He'd practice a while
     Before quittin' his job

But he would be back
     He knew full well
'Cause he had one more story
     He needed to tell

The Elevator

Bob was tired of hearin' his wife
  Complainin' and a whinin'
About goin' to the city
  For some shoppin' and some dinin'

So he thought he'd haul her into town
  And Little Bob as well
Maybe that would quiet her down
  And settle her for a spell

So they loaded up in the pickup
  Little Bob in the back
Him and Spot the cow dog
  Settin' on a gunny sack

They headed into town
  Her hair was fixed just right
Though Bob said she was always prettier
  Before full daylight

"Look hon" she said
  With a squall
"There's one of them there
  shoppin' malls"

So like a good husband
  Bob shopped by her side
Only once or twice
  Contemplatin' suicide

Until she says, "I need to get
  Some lingerie"
He said, "I need to get
  Little Bob away"

So they wandered down
  To the end of the hall
Right there in that
  Shoppin' mall

And there was two double doors
      Without no knobs
Just plain stumped
      Both the Bobs

Numbers there
      Above the door
Went from one
      Plumb up to four

Then an ugly old woman
      As ugly as sin
Poked on a button
      And walked right in

This a little room
      'Bout six foot square
And he reckoned she stood
      There weren't no chair

The numbers rose
      Plumb to the top
Then slowly they
      Began to drop

Open again
      The doors they yawned
And out stepped
      This gorgeous blond

Well. Bob's chin it dropped
      His mouth it drooled
He thought maybe
      He'd been fooled

He said, "We gotta try this
      On another
Hurry son
      Go fetch your mother"

The Drought of "02"

I wonder how much of our civilization now days realize how critical moisture is to our farming and ranching communities. It's a hard thing to see a ranch, that has been in the family for generations, being sold due to the lack of rain. It takes a special breed of man and woman who not only are willing to face the challenges of farming and ranching but love the life on the land. I cringe when I hear the weatherman say, "It's gonna' be a great day for golfin'", which when translated means "No moisture in the forecast."

The Drought of "02"

He sets in the saddle
      As they load out the cattle
The last load goes today

They fought to the end
      The drought and the wind
As he watches the trucks pull away

Then he feels his heart swell
      As there in the corral
He watches his son, and his son

Cowboys at heart
      Each doin' his part
Now their cowboyin' days may be done

'Cause the cattle's been shipped
      The boys are tight lipped
Wonderin' if their futures done wrote

There's not much to say
      There's bill we can't pay
And the bank is holdin' the note

Six generations of men
      Since grandad began
This ranch here on the plains

After all these years
Now it appears
We'll lose it from the lack of the rains

'Cause there's taxes to pay
Still owe for some hay
The bank has a note on the cattle

He thinks of the brand
And the blood in the land
As he hears that last gate rattle

Then there's nothin' to say
As the boys ride away
Each thinkin' thoughts of their own

It's like buryin' a friend
Who rode to his end
And left you feelin' alone

Now with the passin' of time
I'd like this rhyme
To have a happy end

But the drought's still here
Winters right near
All I hear is the cold north wind

Now more time has passed
            Winters came fast
The temperature drops on down

It cuts to the bone
            He's ridin' all alone
The boys have all moved to town

He saddles each day
            Which was always his way
Though its near twenty below

There's nothin' but cold
            And he's been told
It's so dry it just can't snow

He remembers the bible he read
            The words that it said
Things in this world just won't last

As he sets in the saddle
            He can still smell the cattle
And his dreams are dreams of the past

Riding for the Brand

The first poem I wrote years ago. I reckon it will always be my favorite.

An old cowboy and a preacher
    Met on the prairie one day
One ridin' a buckskin
    The other a bay

They squatted in the shade
    Of a lone cedar tree
Scratchin' the dirt with a stick
    Contemplatin' you see

Comparing their lives
    The old cowboy he spoke
Of the brands he'd rid for
    And the horses he'd broke

Of the herds he had gathered
    And held at all cost
Of hours spent ridin'
    When a few head were lost

You'd give up your life
    When you rode for the brand
'Cause of this we buried
    Many a good hand

But as you can see
    I'm well past my prime
Boss says soon
    I'll have to draw up my time

What can I do
    I'm too tough to cry
But I'm too old to work
    And too young to die

Well the preacher stirred the dirt
 With his stick for a while
Then he looked the old cowboy
 In the eye with a smile

He said, I too
 Ride for the brand
The scars are the nail holes
 In the palms of his hands

I've gathered a herd
 And hold for my boss
I'm always out lookin'
 For those who are lost

And many have died
 Who rode for this brand
We all may be called on
 To take up a stand

But you're never too old
 To ride with my crew
When you sign on here
 You're made as if new

Well, the old cowboy that day
 Hired on for a new boss
And his foreman's the one
 Who died on the cross

And he can ride happy
 To the end of his days
'Cause there's no end to the gather
 Of the lost and the strays

The Blessing

May the Lord up there above
Smile upon you with his love
And may a gentle breeze cross your trail today

Not enough to kick up dust
Or to moan and blow and gust
Just enough to keep the gnats blown away

Should the lightening start to flicker
May you always have your slicker
And a place to hole up from the blow

May your cabin be chinked tight
And your wood stove glowin' bright
To chase away the chill of the winter snow

May your grub be beef and beans
Let the cattle eat the greens
And may your coffee pot never run dry

May you leave tracks on many snows
While peace and happiness flows
Like the eagles as they fly in the sky

ABOUT THE AUTHOR

Bill Bunting was born and raised on a ranch his grandfather homesteaded in the canyon lands of Southeastern Colorado. Born on the prairie he has always had a love for the wide-open spaces. Having a strong interest in the history of Native Americans and the West much of his art as well as his poetry speak of times long past. A prolific writer Bill writes a weekly newspaper column titled "Behind the Grindstone". A firm believer that "Laughter is good medicine" Bill has a unique sense of humor much of which is put to rhyme. Bill and his wife Cheryl have traveled extensively helping start and support cowboy churches. He and his wife live on a small ranch on the High Plains of Southeastern Colorado.